Poems 1962-1978

POEMS
1962-1978

DEREK
MAHON

OXFORD NEW YORK TORONTO MELBOURNE
OXFORD UNIVERSITY PRESS
1979

Oxford University Press, Walton Street, Oxford OX2 6DP

OXFORD LONDON GLASGOW NEW YORK
TORONTO MELBOURNE WELLINGTON KUALA LUMPUR
SINGAPORE HONG KONG TOKYO DELHI
BOMBAY CALCUTTA MADRAS KARACHI
NAIROBI DAR ES SALAAM CAPE TOWN

British Library Catalogue in Publication Data

Mahon, Derek

Poems, 1962–1978.
821′.9′14   PR6063.A34A17   79–40793
ISBN 0–19–211898–6
ISBN 0–19–211897–8 Pbk

Printed in Great Britain by
The Bowering Press Ltd, Plymouth and London

For Doreen;
and for Rory and Katherine
when the time comes

Acknowledgements

Acknowledgements are due to the editors of *Aquarius, The New Statesman, The Poetry Review, The Honest Ulsterman, Hibernia, The Irish Times, New Irish Writing, Ciphers, Magill,* and *Ploughshares,* where some of the most recent poems first appeared; and to the BBC and RTE. 'Light Music' was originally published in pamphlet form by Ulsterman Publications (Belfast) and 'The Sea in Winter' by Gallery Books (Dublin and Deerfield, Mass.). I would like to acknowledge the generous assistance of the Arts Councils of Great Britain and Ireland.

Contents

Glengormley

'Wonders are many and none is more wonderful than
                                                    man'
Who has tamed the terrier, trimmed the hedge
And grasped the principle of the watering-can.
Clothes-pegs litter the window ledge
And the long ships lie in clover. Washing lines
Shake out white linen over the chalk thanes.

Now we are safe from monsters, and the giants
Who tore up sods twelve miles by six
And hurled them out to sea to become islands
Can worry us no more. The sticks
And stones that once broke bones will not now harm
A generation of such sense and charm.

Only words hurt us now. No saint or hero,
Landing at night from the conspiring seas,
Brings dangerous tokens to the new era—
Their sad names linger in the histories.
The unreconciled, in their metaphysical pain,
Dangle from lamp-posts in the dawn rain;

And much dies with them. I should rather praise
A worldly time under this worldly sky—
The terrier-taming, garden-watering days
Those heroes pictured as they struggled through
The quick noose of their finite being. By
Necessity, if not choice, I live here too.

The Poets of the Nineties

Slowly, with the important carelessness
Of your kind, each spirit-sculptured face
Appears before me, eyes
Bleak from discoveries.

I had almost forgotten you had been,
So jealous was I of my skin
And the world with me. How
Goes it with you now?

Did death and its transitions disappoint you,
And the worms you so looked forward to?
Perhaps you found that you had to *queue*
For a ticket into hell,
Despite your sprays of laurel.

You were all children in your helpless wisdom,
Retiring loud-mouths who would not be dumb—
Frustrated rural clergymen
Nobody would ordain.

Then ask no favour of reincarnation,
No yearning after the booze and whores—
For you, if anyone,
Have played your part
In holding nature up to art . . .

Be content to sprawl in your upland meadows,
Hair and boy-mouths stuck with flowers—
And rest assured, the day
Will be all sunlight, and the night
A dutiful spectrum of stars.

In Carrowdore Churchyard
at the grave of Louis MacNeice

Your ashes will not stir, even on this high ground,
However the wind tugs, the headstones shake.
This plot is consecrated, for your sake,
To what lies in the future tense. You lie
Past tension now, and spring is coming round
Igniting flowers on the peninsula.

Your ashes will not fly, however the rough winds burst
Through the wild brambles and the reticent trees.
All we may ask of you we have. The rest
Is not for publication, will not be heard.
Maguire, I believe, suggested a blackbird
And over your grave a phrase from Euripides.

Which suits you down to the ground, like this church-
    yard
With its play of shadow, its humane perspective.
Locked in the winter's fist, these hills are hard
As nails, yet soft and feminine in their turn
When fingers open and the hedges burn.
This, you implied, is how we ought to live—

The ironical, loving crush of roses against snow,
Each fragile, solving ambiguity. So
From the pneumonia of the ditch, from the ague
Of the blind poet and the bombed-out town you bring
The all-clear to the empty holes of spring;
Rinsing the choked mud, keeping the colours new.

The Spring Vacation
for Michael Longley

Walking among my own this windy morning
In a tide of sunlight between shower and shower,
I resume my old conspiracy with the wet
Stone and the unwieldy images of the squinting heart.
Once more, as before, I remember not to forget.

There is a perverse pride in being on the side
Of the fallen angels and refusing to get up.
We could *all* be saved by keeping an eye on the hill
At the top of every street, for there it is,
Eternally, if irrelevantly, visible—

But yield instead to the humorous formulae,
The hidden menace in the knowing nod.
Or we keep sullen silence in light and shade,
Rehearsing our astute salvations under
The cold gaze of a sanctimonious God.

One part of my mind must learn to know its place.
The things that happen in the kitchen houses
And echoing back-streets of this desperate city
Should engage more than my casual interest,
Exact more interest than my casual pity.

4

Grandfather

They brought him in on a stretcher from the world,
Wounded but humorous. And he soon recovered.
Boiler-rooms, row upon row of gantries rolled
Away to reveal the landscape of a childhood
Only he can recapture. Even on cold
Mornings he is up at six with a block of wood
Or a box of nails, discreetly up to no good
Or banging round the house like a four-year-old—

Never there when you call. But after dark
You hear his great boots thumping in the hall
And in he comes, as cute as they come. Each night
His shrewd eyes bolt the door and set the clock
Against the future, then his light goes out.
Nothing escapes him; he escapes us all.

My Wicked Uncle

His was the first corpse I had ever seen,
Untypically silent in the front room.
Death had deprived him of his moustache,
His thick horn-rimmed spectacles,
The easy corners of his salesman dash—
Those things by which I had remembered him—
And sundered him behind a sort of gauze.
His hair was badly parted on the right
As if for Sunday School. That night
I saw my uncle as he really was.

5

The stories he retailed were mostly
Wicked-avuncular fantasy;
He went in for waistcoats and Brylcreem.
But something about him
Demanded that you picture the surprise
Of the Chairman of the Board, when to
'What will you have with your whiskey?' my uncle re-
    plies,
'Another whiskey please.'

He claimed to have been arrested in New York
Twice on the same day—
The crookedest chief steward in the Head Line.
And once, so he would say,
Sailing from San Francisco to Shanghai,
He brought a crew of lascars out on strike
In protest at the loss of a day's pay
Crossing the International Dateline.

He was buried on a blustery day above the sea,
The young Presbyterian minister
Tangled and wind-swept in the sea air.
I saw sheep huddled in the long wet grass
Of the golf course, and the empty freighters
Sailing for ever down Belfast Lough
In a fine rain, their sirens going,
As the gradual graph of my uncle's life
And times dipped precipitately
Into the black earth of Carnmoney Cemetery.

His teenage kids are growing horns and claws—
More wicked already than ever my uncle was.

The Death of Marilyn Monroe

If it were said, let there be no more light,
Let rule the wide winds and the long-tailed seas,
Then she would die in all our hearts tonight—
Till when, her image broods over the cities
In negative, for in the darkness she is bright,
Caught in a pose of infinite striptease.

Goddesses, from the whipped sea or the slums,
Will understand her final, desolate
Stark-nakedness, her teeth ground to the gums,
Fingernails filthy, siren hair in spate;
And always with her, as she goes and comes,
Her little bottle of barbiturate—

For she was one of them, queen among the trash,
Cinders swept to the palace from her shack
By some fairy godmother; in a flash
Spirited to the front row from the back.
Stars last so long before they go scattering ash
Down the cold back-streets of the Zodiac;

Fall and dissolve into the thickening air,
Burning the black ground of the negative.
We are slowly learning from meteors like her
Who have learnt how to shrivel and let live
That when an immovable body meets an ir-
resistible force, something has got to give.

Preface to a Love Poem

This is a circling of itself and you—
A form of words, compact and compromise,
    Prepared in the false dawn of the half-true
Beyond which the shapes of truth materialize.
    This is a blind with sunlight filtering through.

This is a stirring in the silent hours,
As lovers do with thoughts they cannot frame
    Or leave, but bring to darkness like night-flowers,
Words never choosing but the words choose them—
    Birds crowing, wind whistling off pale stars.

This is a night-cry, neither here nor there—
A ghostly echo from the clamorous dead
    Who cried aloud in anger and despair
Outlasting stone and bronze, but took instead
    Their lost grins underground with them for ever.

This is at one remove, a substitute
For final answers; but the wise man knows
    To cleave to the one living absolute
Beyond paraphrase, and shun a shrewd repose.
    The words are aching in their own pursuit

To say 'I love you' out of indolence,
As one might speak at sea without forethought,
    Drifting inconsequently among islands.
This is a way of airing my distraught
    Love of your silence. You are the soul of silence.

Bird Sanctuary
for Jill Schlesinger

Towards sleep I came
Upon the place again,
Its muted sea and tame
Eddying wind. The mist and rain
Come only after dark, and then
Steam out to sea at dawn.

There I have erected
A bird sanctuary to hold
The loaded world in check.
This is where all my birds collect—
Cormorant, puffin and kittiwake
All duly enrolled.

I live elsewhere—
In a city down the coast
Composed of earth and fire.
At night I walk beside the river
So that the elements of air
And water are not lost.

I expect great things
Of these angels of wind,
Females, males and fledgelings.
The sudden whirring of their wings
Disturbs the noon, and midnight rings
With echoes from their island.

There will come a time
When they sit on the housetops
Shouting, thousands of them,
This is their own, their favourite dream
Beyond reason, beyond rhyme,
So that the heart stops.

A Mythological Figure

There ought to have been a mythological figure
Condemned always to sing whenever
She opened her mouth to speak. The gods,
Perhaps, had frowned upon
A too familiar attitude in her,
An implied inkling of their random methods,
But let her live because she was a woman.
Then she began to sing, and her gestures
Flowed like a mountain stream;
But her songs were without words,
Or the words without meaning—
Like the cries of love or the cries of mourning.

De Quincey at Grasmere

Tonight the blessed state, that long repose
Where time is measured
Not by the clock but by the hours
Of the wind. His seventh heaven when it snows
The valley under, and the frosty stars
Sing to his literary leisure.

Hearth rugs, a tea pot and a quart
Decanter of laudanum—
Perihelion of paradise! No sort
Or condition of men but is the less human
For want of this. *Mens sana*
In corpore sano.

Excellent as an antidote for toothache
And the busy streets. Wood crackles better
In a head removed, and fresh water
Springs wiselier in a heart that is not sick.
And then the dreams came, and his children
Woke him every day at noon—

Until he cried out, 'I will sleep no more!'
And quit the hot sheets and the enormous
Apparitions dying on the floor.
He left the house,
Walked out to the sunlight on the hill
And heard, in the whispering-gallery of his soul,

His own, small, urgent discord echoing back
From dark roads taken at random
And the restless thunder of London—
Where he had gone in his eighteenth year
And wandered Soho after dark
With Anne, looking for some such panacea.

Breton Walks

1 *Early Morning*
No doubt the creation was something like this—
A cold day breaking on silent stones,
Slower than time, spectacular only in size.
First there is darkness, then somehow light,
We call this day and the other night
And watch in vain for the second of sunrise.

Suddenly, near at hand, the click of a wooden shoe—
An old woman among the primeval shapes,
Abroad in the field of light, sombrely dressed.
She calls good-day, since there are bad days too,
And her eyes go down. She has seen perhaps
Ten thousand dawns like this, and is not impressed.

2 *Man and Bird*
All fly away at my approach
As they have done time out of mind,
And hide in the thicker leaves to watch
The shadowy ingress of mankind.

My whistle-talk fails to disarm
Presuppositions of ill-will;
Although they rarely come to harm
The ancient fear is in them still.

Which irritates my *amour propre*
As an enlightened alien
And renders yet more wide the gap
From their world to the world of men.

So perhaps they have something after all—
Either we shoot them out of hand
Or parody them with a bird-call
Neither of us can understand.

3 *After Midnight*
They are all round me in the dark
With claw-knives for my sleepy anarch—

Beasts of the field, birds of the air,
Their slit-eyes glittering everywhere.

I am man self-made, self-made man,
No small-talk now for those who ran

In and out of my dirty childhood.
We have grown up as best we could.

Lost traveller, by a hunter's moon
They will gnaw your history to the bone.

4 *Exit Molloy*
Now at the end I smell the smells of spring
Where in a dark ditch I lie wintering—
And the little town only a mile away,
Happy and fatuous in the light of day.
A bell tolls gently. I should start to cry
But my eyes are closed and my face dry.
I am not important and I have to die.
Strictly speaking I am already dead
But still I can hear the birds sing on over my head.

Van Gogh in the Borinage
for Colin Middleton

Shivering in the darkness
Of pits, slag heaps, beetroot fields,
I gasp for light and life
Like a caged bird in springtime
Banging the bright bars.

Like a glow-worm I move among
The caged Belgian miners,
And the light on my forehead
Is the dying light of faith.
God gutters down to metaphor—

A subterranean tapping, light
Refracted in a glass of beer
As if through a church window,
Or a basin ringed with coal dust
After the evening bath.

Theo, I am discharged for being
Over-zealous, they call it,
And not dressing the part.
In time I shall go south
And paint what I have seen—

A meteor of golden light
On chairs, faces and old boots,
Setting fierce fire to the eyes
Of sunflowers and fishing boats,
Each one a miner in disguise.

The Forger

When I sold my fake Vermeers to Goering
Nobody knew, nobody guessed
The agony, the fanaticism
Of working beyond criticism
And better than the best.

When they hauled me before the war-crimes tribunal
No one suspected, nobody knew
The agony of regrets
With which I told my secrets.
They missed the point, of course—
To hell with the national heritage,
I sold my *soul* for potage.

The experts were good value, though,
When they went to work on my studio—
Not I, but *they* were the frauds.
I revolutionized their methods.

Now, nothing but claptrap
About 'mere technique' and 'true vision',
As if there were a distinction—
Their way of playing it down.
But my genius will live on;
For even at one remove
The thing I meant was love.

And I too have wandered
In the dark streets of Holland
With hunger at my belly
When the mists rolled in from the sea;

And I too have suffered
Obscurity and derision,
And sheltered in my heart of hearts
A light to transform the world.

Jail Journal

For several days I have been under
House arrest. My table has become
A sun-dial to its empty bottle.
With wise abandon
Lover and friend have gone.

In the window opposite
An old lady sits each afternoon
Talking to no one. I shout.
Either she is deaf or
She has reason.

I have books, provisions, running water
And a little stove. It wouldn't matter
If cars moved silently at night
And no light or laughter
Came from the houses down the street.

It is taking longer than almost anything—
But I know, when it is over
And back come friend and lover,
I shall forget it like a childhood illness
Or a sleepless night-crossing.

Day Trip to Donegal

We reached the sea in early afternoon,
Climbed stiffly out. There were things to be done,
Clothes to be picked up, friends to be seen.
As ever, the nearby hills were a deeper green
Than anywhere in the world, and the grave
Grey of the sea the grimmer in that enclave.

Down at the pier the boats gave up their catch,
Torn mouths and spewed-up lungs. They fetch
Ten times as much in the city as there,
And still the fish come in year after year—
Herring and whiting, flopping about the deck
In attitudes of agony and heartbreak.

We left at eight, drove back the way we came,
The sea receding down each muddy lane.
Around midnight we changed-down into suburbs
Sunk in a sleep no gale-force wind disturbs.
The time of year had left its mark
On frosty pavements glistening in the dark.

Give me a ring, goodnight, and so to bed . . .
That night the slow sea washed against my head,
Performing its immeasurable erosions—
Spilling into the skull, marbling the stones
That spine the very harbour wall,
Muttering its threat to villages of landfall.

At dawn I was alone far out at sea
Without skill or reassurance (nobody
To show me how, no promise of rescue)
Cursing my failure to take due
Forethought for this; contriving vain
Overtures to the mindless wind and rain.

September in Great Yarmouth

The woodwind whistles down the shore
Piping the stragglers home; the gulls
Snaffle and bolt their final mouthfuls.
Only the youngsters call for more.

Chimneys breathe and beaches empty,
Everyone queues for the inland cold—
Middle-aged parents growing old
And teenage kids becoming twenty.

Now the first few spots of rain
Spatter the sports page in the gutter.
Council workmen stab the litter.
You have sown and reaped; now sow again.

The band packs in, the banners drop,
The ice-cream stiffens in its cone.
The boatman lifts his megaphone:
'Come in, fifteen, your time is up.'

An Unborn Child

I have already come to the verge of
Departure. A month or so and
I shall be vacating this familiar room.
Its fabric fits me like a glove
While leaving latitude for a free hand.
I begin to put on the manners of the world,
Sensing the splitting light above
My head, where in the silence I lie curled.

Certain mysteries are relayed to me
Through the dark network of my mother's body
While she sits sewing the white shrouds
Of my apotheosis. I know the twisted
Kitten that lies there sunning itself
Under the bare bulb, the clouds
Of goldfish mooning around upon the shelf.
In me these data are already vested;

I feel them in my bones—bones which embrace
Nothing, for I am completely egocentric.
The pandemonium of encumbrances
Which will absorb me, mind and senses—
Intricacies of the box and the rat-race—
I imagine only. Though they linger and,
Like fingers, stretch until the knuckles crack,
They cannot dwarf the dimensions of my hand.

I must compose myself in the nerve-centre
Of this metropolis, and not fidget—
Although sometimes at night, when the city
Has gone to sleep, I keep in touch with it,
Listening to the warm red water
Racing in the sewers of my mother's body;
Or the moths, soft as eyelids, or the rain
Wiping its wet wings on the window-pane.

And sometimes too, in the small hours of the morning
When the dead filament has ceased to ring,
After the goldfish are dissolved in darkness
And the kitten has gathered itself up into a ball
Between the groceries and the sewing,
I slip the trappings of my harness
To range these hollows in discreet rehearsal
And, battering at the concavity of my caul,

Produce in my mouth the words 'I want to live!'—
This my first protest, and shall be my last.
As I am innocent, everything I do
Or say is couched in the affirmative.
I want to see, hear, touch and taste
These things with which I am to be encumbered.
Perhaps I needn't worry. Give
Or take a day or two, my days are numbered.

The Condensed Shorter Testament
after Villon

In the year fourteen fifty-six
(Black-and-white January weather,
Wolves howling at night sometimes)
The peccant author of these lines,
Ceasing to kick against the pricks
And acting on an urge to break
The yoke of love around his neck,
Decided to pull himself together.

So I do what I think is best
Since she, with no thought of disguise,
Observes with little interest
The desperate longing in my eyes—
Which makes my bowels cry to heaven
For succour from those gods above
Whose function is to shield the stricken
Lover from the knives of love.

And if I chose to misconstrue
A casual word or lingering glance
That charged my body through and through
As having some significance,
I have surely learnt my lesson now;
My heart is torn out by the root.
Now I must look elsewhere and put
Some other pasture to the plough.

And since I have no choice but to go
And cannot vouch for my return
(I am not above reproach, I know,
Not being cast in bronze or iron;
Life is unsure, and death, we learn,
Brings no relief in any event),
For all those whom it may concern
I make this will and testament.

To the bad bitch who, as I said,
So negligently discarded me
That now I feel my senses dead,
All 'pleasure' imbecility,
I leave my heart, an empty bag
For her to play with when it rains.
Although she treats me like a dog
God grant her the mercy she disdains.

To my old cronies of the street,
Anonymous lest these lines be brought
To the keen eyes of the police,
I leave my sword of finest steel
Which in a certain pawnshop lies;
That they may claim it, if they will,
Before the monthly sale takes place
And use it on the creeps and spies.

Out of compassion I would leave
To children starving in the snow
Something to bring them some relief;
But a kind thought will have to do.
God help them, not a shirt nor shoe
To clothe their naked suffering!
If only I could help them through
At least into the coming spring . . .

To the landlord, when I depart,
I leave my dog-eared Aristotle,
Most of which I know by heart;
Also an empty brandy bottle,
And the few rags remaining when
He knocks the door to find me gone—
Cast-offs of a defaulting tenant
Which he may keep in lieu of rent.

Well, I had got so far tonight,
Alone in the silence of my room
And being in the mood to write,
When interrupted by the boom
Of the great clock in the Sorbonne
Announcing midnight to the streets,
And set aside these scribbled sheets
To pray, as I have always done.

When my devotions after a while
Grew still, and the mind, to my relief,
Returned, I turned again to the will
But found my inkwell frozen stiff
And my last candle burnt away—
So, muffled up in cloak and hat,
I closed my eyes to sleep till day
And let my testament go at that.

Done at the aforesaid time of year
By Villon, of such great repute
He wastes away with cold and hunger,
Thin as a rake and black as soot.
All his possessions, castle and court,
To various friends are given away—
All but a little change, and that
Will scarcely last beyond today.

Girls in their Seasons

Girls in their seasons. Solstice and equinox,
This year, make reincarnate
Spry ghosts I had consigned to fate,
Left soaking at the ends of bars,
Pasted in dying calendars
Or locked in clocks.

I can no longer walk the streets at night
But under a lamp-post by a bistro,
To the sound of a zither,
I see one standing in an arc of snow,
Her collar up against the wintry weather,
Smoking a cigarette.

Or, as now, slumped by a train window,
The hair of another flies in the slipstream.
This one is here in an advisory
Capacity, reminding me
Of a trip I took last winter
From dream into bad dream.

Their ghosts go with me as I hurtle north
Into the night,
Gathering momentum, age,
Know-how, experience (I travel light)—
Girls, you are welcome to my luggage
For what it is worth.

No earthly schedule can predict
Accurately our several destinations.
All we can do is wash and dress
And keep ourselves intact.
Besides which, this is an express
And passes all the stations.

Now we are running out of light and love,
Having left far behind
By-pass and fly-over.
The moon is no longer there
And matches go out in the wind.
Now all we have

Is the flinty chink of Orion and the Plough
And the incubators of a nearby farm
To light us through to the Land of Never-Never.
Girls all, be with me now
And keep me warm
Before we go plunging into the dark for ever.

Canadian Pacific

From famine, pestilence and persecution
Those gaunt forefathers shipped abroad to find
Rough stone of heaven beyond the western ocean,
And staked their claim, and pinned their faith.
Tonight their children whistle through the dark;
Frost chokes the windows. They will not have heard
The wild geese flying south over the lakes
While the lakes harden beyond grief and anger—
The eyes fanatical, rigid the soft necks,
The great wings sighing with a nameless hunger.

Epitaph for Robert Flaherty
(after reading *The Innocent Eye*, by Arthur
Calder-Marshall, in Montreal, Canada)

The relief to be out of the sun,
To have come north once more
To my islands of dark ore
Where winter is so long
Only a little light
Gets through, and that perfect.

April on Toronto Island

I go down once more to the island
On the first morning of spring.
The boardwalks are silent
And silent the locked churches.
A last wintry reluctance
Clutches the splintered birches.

Having spent an entire winter
In this night of a country
And gazed at an icy sunset
From the roof of the CBC,
I consider myself an expert
On Pascal's 'infinite spaces'.

There is silence among the houses
And silence along the shore
With its litter of tin cans
And oily fish-skeletons.
There is not even a bird
Although there are bird voices.

But slowly, in ones and twos,
The people are coming back
To stand on the thin beach among
The flotsam of the winter
And watch the grain-ships moving
Eastward to the St Lawrence.

Their faces dream of other islands,
Clear cliffs and salt water,
Fields brighter than paradise
In the first week of creation—
Redemption in a wind or a tide,
Our lives in infinite preparation.

Thinking of Inishere in Cambridge, Massachusetts
for Eamon Grennan

A dream of limestone in sea light
Where gulls have placed their perfect prints.
Reflection in that final sky
Shames vision into simple sight;
Into pure sense, experience.
Atlantic leagues away tonight,
Conceived beyond such innocence,
I clutch the memory still, and I
Have measured everything with it since.

Homecoming

Has bath and shave,
clean shirt etcetera,
full of potatoes,
rested, yet
badly distraught
by six-hour flight
(Boston to Dublin)
drunk all night
with crashing bore
from Houston, Tex.,
who spoke at length
on guns and sex.
Bus into town
and, sad to say,
no change from when
he went away

two years ago.
Goes into bar,
affixes gaze
on evening star.
Skies change but not
souls change. Behold
this is the way
the world grows old.
Scientists, birds,
we cannot start
at this late date
with a pure heart,
or having seen
the pictures plain
be ever innocent again.

A Kind of People

Umbrellas and parasols,
Like old navy raincoats,
Sewing machines, bird-baths,
Shovels and violins,
Are really a kind of people.
(Renoir discovered this.)

They look after their own,
They love one another;
Sky-blue and olive-green
They all flock together,
Jostling on spring pavements
And autumn promenades.

Stripped down in tool-sheds
Or behind basement boilers,
We know they have also shivered
In the cold draught of despair
And are, therefore, the more
Ecstatic after rain—

After a light sun-shower
When they are clean and new,
Taut linen drenched with sunlight
Like water on rose-petals
Or water on bare shoulders
Emerging from the sea.

The Poets Lie Where They Fell

There is no rest for the wicked.
Curled up in armchairs
Or flat out on the floors
Of well-furnished apartments
Belonging to friends of friends,
We lie where we fell.

One more shiftless habit,
It joins the buttered books,
Stale loaves and wandering dishes,
The shirts in the oven
And the volcanic ashtray.
Forgive us, this is our way;

We were born to this—
Deckchairs, train corridors,
American bus stations,
Park benches, open boats,
And wind-worried terraces
Of nineteenth-century Paris.

Forgive us, we mean well
To your wives' well-wrought ankles,
Their anthropomorphic shoes.
We love your dying embers,
Your happy moonstruck bottles,
And we lie where we fell.

Back home in mid-morning
We wash, we change and drink
Coffee, perhaps we sing.
Then off we go once more,
Smiling our secret smile and only
Slightly the worse for wear.

A Dying Art

'That day would skin a fairy—
A dying art,' she said.
Not many left of the old trade.
Redundant and remote, they age
Gracefully in dark corners
With lamplighters, sailmakers
And native Manx speakers.

And the bone-handled knives with which
They earned their bread? My granny grinds
Her plug tobacco with one to this day.

Ecclesiastes

God, you could grow to love it, God-fearing, God-
    chosen purist little puritan that,
for all your wiles and smiles, you are (the
    dank churches, the empty streets,
the shipyard silence, the tied-up swings) and
    shelter your cold heart from the heat
of the world, from woman-inquisition, from the
    bright eyes of children. Yes you could
wear black, drink water, nourish a fierce zeal
    with locusts and wild honey, and not
feel called upon to understand and forgive
    but only to speak with a bleak
afflatus, and love the January rains when they
    darken the dark doors and sink hard
into the Antrim hills, the bog meadows, the heaped
    graves of your fathers. Bury that red
bandana and stick, that banjo; this is your
    country, close one eye and be king.
Your people await you, their heavy washing
    flaps for you in the housing estates—
a credulous people. God, you could do it, God
    help you, stand on a corner stiff
with rhetoric, promising nothing under the sun.

Teaching in Belfast

Brightness of brightness shimmers and is gone;
The music founders to the cries of children,
Screaming of bells, the rattle of milk bottles,
Footfall echoes of jails and hospitals.

I think I have been sitting here half my life,
Feet on desk, drumming a confiscated penknife
On a pile of unsatisfactory homework.
Careful, kids; my bite is worse than my bark.
I love them, but not even the greatest lover
Can stay on form five days a week for ever
And not start reading, over the loved head,
Book titles on the shelf behind the bed.
At five to two the lunch hour nears its end
And gulls come down on the deserted playground,
One at a time, to search the litter bins.
This is the moment my fantasy begins
And I drive with a generous lady, long since lost,
Against the traffic to the glittering west,
Startling the hens in drowsy villages,
Cushioned with money, time and privileges.
O chalky teachers, you would gladly do
Without your pensions to be with me too!
The fields are bright with sunlight after rain,
The skies are clear, the music starts again . . .

Bruce Ismay's Soliloquy

They said I got away in a boat
And humbled me at the inquiry. I tell you
    I sank as far that night as any
Hero. As I sat shivering on the dark water
    I turned to ice to hear my costly
Life go thundering down in a pandemonium of
    Prams, pianos, sideboards, winches,
Boilers bursting and shredded ragtime. Now I hide
    In a lonely house behind the sea
Where the tide leaves broken toys and hatboxes

Silently at my door. The showers of
April, flowers of May mean nothing to me, nor the
    Late light of June, when my gardener
Describes to strangers how the old man stays in bed
    On seaward mornings after nights of
Wind, and will see no one, repeat no one. Then it is
    I drown again with all those dim
Lost faces I never understood. My poor soul
    Screams out in the starlight, heart
Breaks loose and rolls down like a stone.
    Include me in your lamentations.

The Studio

You would think with so much going on outside
The deal table would make for the window,
The ranged crockery freak and wail
Remembering its dark origins, the frail
Oilcloth, in a fury of recognitions,
Disperse in a thousand directions,
And the simple bulb in the ceiling, honed
By death to a worm of pain, to a hair
Of heat, to a light snowflake laid
In a dark river at night—and wearied
Above all by the life-price of time
And the failure by only a few tenths
Of an inch but completely and for ever
Of the ends of a carefully drawn equator
To meet, sing and be one—abruptly
Roar into the floor.
                    But it
Never happens like that. Instead
There is this quivering silence

In which, day by day, the play
Of light and shadow (shadow mostly)
Repeats itself, though never exactly.

This is the all-purpose bed-, work- and bedroom.
Its mourning faces are cracked porcelain only quicker,
Its knuckles door-knobs only lighter,
Its occasional cries of despair
A function of the furniture.

In the Aran Islands
for Tom and Peggy MacIntyre

He is earthed to his girl, one hand fastened
In hers, and with his free hand listens,
An earphone, to his own rendition,
Singing the darkness into the light.
I close the pub door gently and step out
Into the yard, and the song goes out,
And a gull creaks off from the tin roof
Of an outhouse, planing over the ocean,
Circling now with a hoarse inchoate
Screaming the boned fields of its vision.
God, that was the way to do it,
Hand-clasping, echo-prolonging poet!

Scorched with a fearful admiration
Walking over the nacreous sand,
I dream myself to that tradition,
Fifty winters off the land—
One hand to an ear for the vibration,
The far wires, the reverberation
Down light-years of the imagination
And, in the other hand, your hand.

The long glow leaps from the dark soil, however—
No marsh-light holds a candle to this.
Unearthly still in its white weather
A crack-voiced rock-marauder, scavenger, fierce
Friend to no slant fields or the sea either,
Folds back over the forming waters.

Rocks
after Guillevic

The rocks would never recognize
The image of themselves
These lovers entertain,
Lying in their shadows
In the last traces of time.

All they know is their own
Shuddering endurance,
Their dream of holding fast
In the elemental flux—

Bewildered both in the
Approach and the discovery.

Two Songs

1 *His Song*

Months on, you hold me still;
at dawn, bright-rising like a hill-
horizon, gentle, kind with rain
and the primroses of April.
I shall never know them again
but still your bright shadow
puts out its shadow, daylight, on
the shadows I lie with now.

2 *Her Song*

A hundred men imagine
love when I drink wine;
and then I begin to think
of your words and mine.
The mountain is silent now
where the snow lies fresh,
and my love like the sloe-
blossom on a blackthorn bush.

A Tolerable Wisdom

You keep the cold from the body, the cold from the mind.
Heartscloth, soulswool, without you there would be
Short shrift for the pale beast in a winter's wind.
Too swift exposure by too harsh a sea.
Cold I have known, its sports-pages adrift
Past frozen dodgems in the amusement park,
One crumpled *Gauloise* thumbing a late lift
Where Paris flamed on the defining dark.

You've heard the gravel at the window, seen
A lost figure unmanned by closing-time.
More honour to you that took him in,
Fed buns and cocoa, sweetness, the sought dream
Of warmth and light against your listening skin
And rocked him to a tolerable wisdom.

An Image from Beckett
for Doreen Douglas

In that instant
There was a sea, far off,
As bright as lettuce,

A northern landscape
And a huddle
Of houses along the shore.

Also, I think, a white
Flicker of gulls
And washing hung to dry—

The poignancy of those
Back-yards—and the gravedigger
Putting aside his forceps.

Then the hard boards
And darkness once again.
But in that instant

I was struck
By the sweetness and light,
The sweetness and light,

Imagining what grave
Cities, what lasting monuments,
Given the time.

They will have buried
My great-grandchildren, and theirs,
Beside me by now

With a subliminal batsqueak
Of reflex lamentation.
Our hair and excrement

Litter the rich earth,
Changing, second by second,
To civilizations.

It was good while it lasted,
And if it only lasted
The biblical span

Required to drop six feet
Through a glitter of wintry light,
There is No one to blame.

Still, I am haunted
By that landscape,
The soft rush of its winds,

The uprightness of its
Utilities and schoolchildren—
To whom in my will,

This, I have left my will.
I hope they had time,
And light enough, to read it.

The Early Anthropologists

The early anthropologists
Left traces of their
Lives everywhere—

Gibbering tapes
Nobody can decipher,
Photographs of their ancestors

Shaking spears at the camera
Or fishing black holes
In the polar ice;

Senile data systems,
Computers in their dotage,
Libraries that crumble to the touch.

We look back on them
With respectful amusement.
Perhaps we can learn from them;

For in their very ignorance
They provide an example
From which we might profit.

Their simple ways
Might yet inspire us
In these difficult days—

Even as we hope to inspire
Those who come after
Bearing fruit through the ruins.

Anthropology has carried
Its basket of apples
A long way, and is tired.

Once it studied man,
Now it studies the study of man,
Soon it will study . . .

Like the baking-soda tin inside
The baking-soda tin
Inside the baking-soda tin.

Meanwhile an old peasant,
Not very bright,
Sits on a rock somewhere

Studying the punctual haemorrhage
Of sea and sky,
The galaxies of dust.

It is growing dark.
He hears distant machinery.
The sun sets in the west without remark.

Lives
for Seamus Heaney

First time out
I was a torc of gold
And wept tears of the sun.

That was fun
But they buried me
In the earth two thousand years

Till a labourer
Turned me up with a pick
In eighteen fifty-four

And sold me
For tea and sugar
In Newmarket-on-Fergus.

Once I was an oar
But stuck in the shore
To mark the place of a grave

When the lost ship
Sailed away. I thought
Of Ithaca, but soon decayed.

The time that I liked
Best was when
I was a bump of clay

In a Navaho rug,
Put there to mitigate
The too godlike

Perfection of that
Merely human artifact.
I served my maker well—

He lived long
To be struck down in
Tucson by an electric shock

The night the lights
Went out in Europe
Never to shine again.

So many lives,
So many things to remember!
I was a stone in Tibet,

A tongue of bark
At the heart of Africa
Growing darker and darker . . .

It all seems
A little unreal now,
Now that I am

An anthropologist
With my own
Credit card, dictaphone,

Army surplus boots,
And a whole boatload
Of photographic equipment.

I know too much
To be anything any more;
And if in the distant

Future someone
Thinks he has once been me
As I am today,

Let him revise
His insolent ontology
Or teach himself to pray.

Deaths

Who died nails, key-rings,
Sword hilts and lunulae,
Rose hash, bog-paper
And deciduous forests,
Died again these things,

Rose kites, wolves,
Piranha fish, and bleached
To a white femur
By desert, by dark river,

Fight now for our
Fourth lives with an
Informed, articulate
Fury frightening to the
Unreflecting progenitors

Who crowd our oxygen tents.
What should we fear
Who never lost by dying?
What should we not as,

Gunsmiths, botanists, having
Taken the measure of
Life, death, we comb our
Bright souls for
Whatever the past holds?

Rage for Order

Somewhere beyond the scorched gable end and the
                              burnt-out buses
    there is a poet indulging
        his wretched rage for order—
or not as the case may be; for his
        is a dying art,
    an eddy of semantic scruples
        in an unstructurable sea.

    He is far from his people,
and the fitful glare of his high window is as
        nothing to our scattered glass.

His posture is grandiloquent and deprecating, like this,
        his diet ashes,
his talk of justice and his mother
        the rhetorical device
    of an etiolated emperor—
Nero if you prefer, no mother there.

    '. . . and this in the face of love,
        death, and the wages of the poor . . .'

If he is silent, it is the silence of enforced humility;
    if anxious to be heard, it is the anxiety
        of a last word
when the drums start; for his is a dying art.

Now watch me as I make history. Watch as I tear down
    to build up with a desperate love,
        knowing it cannot be
    long now till I have need of his
        desperate ironies.

Poem Beginning with a Line by Cavafy

It is night and the barbarians have not come.
It was not always so hard;
When the great court flared
With gallowglasses and language difficulty
A man could be a wheelwright and die happy.

We remember oatmeal and mutton,
Harpsong, a fern table for
Wiping your hands on,
A candle of reeds and butter,
The distaste of the rheumatic chronicler,

A barbarous tongue, and herds like cloud-shadow
Roaming the wet hills
When the hills were young,
Whiskery pikemen and their spiky dogs
Preserved in woodcuts and card-catalogues.

Now it is night and the barbarians have not come.
Or if they have we only recognize,
Harsh as a bombed bathroom,
The frantic anthropologisms
And lazarous ironies behind their talk

Of fitted carpets, central heating
And automatic gear-change—
Like the bleached bones of a hare
Or a handful of spent
Cartridges on a deserted rifle range.

As It Should Be

We hunted the mad bastard
Through bog, moorland, rock, to the star-lit west
And gunned him down in a blind yard
Between ten sleeping lorries
And an electricity generator.

Let us hear no idle talk
Of the moon in the Yellow River.
The air blows softer since his departure.

Since his tide burial during school hours
Our kiddies have known no bad dreams.
Their cries echo lightly along the coast.

This is as it should be.
They will thank us for it when they grow up
To a world with method in it.

A Stone Age Figure Far Below
for Bill McCormack

Through heaving heather, fallen stones
From the wrecked piles of burial cairns
As they fly in over the moors—
Racing about in cloud shadow,
A stone age figure far below
Wildly gesticulating as if
He sees, at last, a sign of life
Or damns them to hell-fires.

When they come with poles, binoculars, whistles,
Blankets and flasks, they will find him dead—
Unkempt, authentic, furnace-eyed
And dead, and his heavy flint hearthstones
Littered with dung and animal bones;

Or a local resident out for a walk
In tweeds and a hunting hat. 'You must be
Mad,' he will say, 'to suppose this rock
Could accommodate life indefinitely.
Nobody comes here now but me.'

Consolations of Philosophy

When we start breaking up in the wet darkness
And the rotten boards fall from us, and the ribs
Crack under the constriction of tree roots
And the seasons slip from the fields unknown to us,

Oh, then there will be the querulous complaining
From citizens who had never dreamt of this—
Who, shaken to the bone in their stout boxes
By the latest bright cars, will not inspect them

And, kept awake by the tremors of new building,
Will not be there to comment. When the broken
Wreath bowls are speckled with rain-water
And the grass grows wild for want of a caretaker,

Oh, then a few will remember with delight
The dust gyrating in a shaft of light;
The integrity of pebbles; a sheep's skull
Grinning its patience on a wintry sill.

Gipsies

I have seen the dark police
rocking your caravans
to wreck the crockery
and wry thoughts of peace
you keep there on waste
ground beside motorways
where the snow lies late
(all this on television)
and am ashamed; fed,
clothed, housed and ashamed.
You might be interested
to hear, though, that on
stormy nights our strong
double glazing groans with
foreknowledge of death,
the fridge with a great wound,
and not surprised to know
the fate you have so long
endured is ours also :
the cars are piling up.
I listen to the wind
and file receipts. The heap
of scrap metal in my
garden grows daily.

Entropy

We are holing up here
in the difficult places—
in caves, terminal moraines
and abandoned farmhouses,
the wires cut, the old car
disposing itself for death
among the inscrutable,
earth-inheriting dandelions.
The roads at evening glitter
with ditched bicycles,
at morning with
the bronze shards
of a monumental sculptor
who lived in the big house
before being bought out
by a property speculator.
We are hiding out here
with the old methods—
growing our own,
chasing hares in the rough.
We are not quick enough,
having become heavy and slow
from long urban idling.
The old folks dream on,
their innocence and purpose
a twig, a leaf, eddying in brown
discrepancies of water—
while we, anemones, 'receive
on our bare rock, whatever
nourishment the wash
of the waves may bring'.

I Am Raftery

I am Raftery, hesitant and confused among
the cold-voiced graduate students and inter-
changeable instructors. Were it not for the
nice wives who do the talking I would have
run out of hope some time ago, and of love.
I have traded-in the 'simplistic maunderings'
that made me famous, for a wry dissimulation,
an imagery of adventitious ambiguity dredged
from God knows what polluted underground spring.
Death is near, I have come of age, I doubt if
I shall survive another East Anglian winter.
Scotch please, plenty of water. I am reading
Joyce by touch and it's killing me. Is it
empty pockets I play to? Not on your life,
they ring with a bright inflationary music—
two seminars a week and my own place reserved
in the record library. Look at me now,
my back to the wall, taking my cue
from an idiot disc-jockey between commercials.

Dog Days

'When you stop to consider
The days spent dreaming of a future
And say then, that was my life.'

For the days are long—
From the first milk van
To the last shout in the night,
An eternity. But the weeks go by

Like birds; and the years, the years
Fly past anti-clockwise
Like clock hands in a bar mirror.

Beyond Howth Head
for Jeremy Lewis

The wind that blows these words to you
Bangs nightly off the black-and-blue
Atlantic, hammering in its haste
Dark doors of the declining west
Whose rock-built houses year by year
Collapse, whose strong sons disappear
(No homespun cottage industries'
Embroidered cloths will patch up these

Lost townlands on the crumbling shores
Of Europe), shivers the dim stars
In rain-water, and spins a single
Garage sign behind the shingle.
Fresh from Long Island or Cape Cod
Night music finds the lightning rod
Of young girls coming from a dance
(You thumbs a lift and takes your chance)

And shakes the radios that play
From the Twelve Pins to Dublin Bay
Where, bored to tears by Telefís,
Vox populi vox dei, we reach
With twinkling importunity
For good news on the BBC,
Our heliotropic Birnam Wood
Reflecting an old gratitude.

What can the elders say to this?
For youth must kiss and then must kiss
And so by this declension fall
To write the writing on the wall.
A little learning in a parked
Volkswagen torches down the dark
And soon disperses fogged belief
With an empiric *joie de vivre.*

The pros outweigh the cons that glow
From Beckett's bleak *reductio*—
And who would trade self-knowledge for
A prelapsarian metaphor,
Love-play of the ironic conscience
For a prescriptive innocence?
'Lewde libertie', whose midnight work
Disturbed the peace of Co. Cork

And fired Kilcolman's windows when
The flower of Ireland looked to Spain,
Come back and be with us again!
But take a form that sheds for love
That tight-arsed, convent-bred disdain
The whole wide world knows nothing of;
And flash, an *aisling,* through the dawn
Where Yeats's hill-men still break stone.

The writing on the wall, we know,
Elsewhere was written long ago.
We fumble with the matches while
The hebona behind the smile
Of grammar gets its brisk forensic
Smack in the *realpolitik*
And Denmark's hot iambics pass
To the cool courts of Cambridge, Mass.—

Leaving us, Jeremy, to flick
Blank pages of an empty book
Where the exponential futures lie
Wide to the runways and the sky;
To spin celestial globes of words
Over a foaming pint in Ward's,
Bowed victims of our linear thought
(Though 'booze is bourgeois pot is not')

Rehearsing for the *fin-de-siècle*
Gruff Jeremiads to redirect
Lost youth into the knacker's yard
Of humanistic self-regard;
To praise what will be taken from us,
The memory of Dylan Thomas,
And sign off with a pounding pen
From Seaford or from Cushendun.

I woke this morning (March) to hear
Church bells of Monkstown through the roar
Of waves round the Martello tower
And thought of the swan-sons of Lir
When Kemoc rang the Christian bell
To crack a fourth-dimensional
World picture, never known again,
And changed them back from swans to men.

It calls as oddly through the wild
Eviscerations of the troubled
Channel between us and North Wales
Where Lycid's ghost for ever sails
(Unbosomings of sea-weed, wrack,
Industrial bile, a boot from Blackpool,
Contraceptives deftly tied
With best regards from Merseyside)

And tinkles with as blithe a sense
Of man's cosmic significance
Who wrote his world from broken stone,
Installed his Word God on the throne
And placed, in Co. Clare, a sign:
'Stop here and see the sun go down'.
Meanwhile, for a word's sake, the plastic
Bombs go off around Belfast;

From the unquiet Cyclades
A Greek poet consults the skies
Where sleepless, cold, computed stars
In random sequence light the bars;
And everywhere the ground is thick
With the dead sparrows rhetoric
Demands as fictive sacrifice
To prove its substance in our eyes.

Roaring, its ten-lane highways pitch
Their simple bodies in the ditch
Where once Molloy, uncycled, heard
Thin cries of a surviving bird;
But soon Persephone, re-found
In the cold darkness underground,
Will speak to the woodlands with fine rain
And the ocean to Cynthia once again.

Spring lights the country. From a thousand
Dusty corners, house by house,
From under beds and vacuum cleaners,
Empty Kosangas containers,
Bread bins, car seats, crates of stout,
The first flies cry to be let out,
To cruise a kitchen, find a door
And die clean in the open air

Whose smokeless clarity distils
A chisel's echo in the hills
As if some Noah, weather-wise,
Could read a deluge in clear skies.
But nothing ruffles the wind's breath:
This peace is the sweet peace of death
Or *l'outre-tombe*. Make no noise,
The foxes have quit Clonmacnoise.

I too, uncycled, might exchange,
Since 'we are changed by what we change',
My forkful of the general mess
For hazel-nuts and water-cress
Like one of those old hermits who,
Less virtuous than some, withdrew
From the world-circles women make
To a small island in a lake.

Chomēi at Tōyama, his blanket
Hemp, his character a rank
Not-to-be-trusted river mist,
Events in Kyōto all grist
To the mill of a harsh irony
(Since we are seen by what we see),
Thoreau like ice among the trees
And Spenser, 'far from enemies',

Might serve as models for a while
But to return in greater style.
Centripetal, the hot world draws
Its children in with loving claws
From rock and heather, rain and sleet
With only Kosangas for heat
And spins them at the centre where
They have no time to know despair

c

But still, like Margaret Fuller, must
'Accept the universe' on trust
And offer to a phantom future
Blood and ouns in forfeiture—
Each one, his poor loaf on the sea,
Monstrous before posterity,
Our afterlives a coming true
Of perfect worlds we never knew.

The light that left you streaks the walls
Of Georgian houses, pubs, cathedrals,
Coasters moored below Butt Bridge
And old men at the water's edge
Where Anna Livia, breathing free,
Weeps silently into the sea,
Her small sorrows mingling with
The wandering waters of the earth.

And here I close; for look, across
Dark waves where bell-buoys dimly toss
The Baily winks beyond Howth Head,
And sleep calls from the silent bed;
While the moon drags her kindred stones
Among the rocks and the strict bones
Of the drowned, and I put out the light
On shadows of the encroaching night.

Monkstown, Co. Dublin; March–April 1970
Lingfield, Surrey; March–April 1975

Afterlives
for James Simmons

I
I wake in a dark flat
To the soft roar of the world.
Pigeons neck on the white
Roofs as I draw the curtains
And look out over London
Rain-fresh in the morning light.

This is our element, the bright
Reason on which we rely
For the long-term solutions.
The orators yap, and guns
Go off in a back-street;
But the faith does not die

That in our time these things
Will amaze the literate children
In their non-sectarian schools
And the dark places be
Ablaze with love and poetry
When the power of good prevails.

What middle-class cunts we are
To imagine for one second
That our privileged ideals
Are divine wisdom, and the dim
Forms that kneel at noon
In the city not ourselves.

2

I am going home by sea
For the first time in years.
Somebody thumbs a guitar
On the dark deck, while a gull
Dreams at the masthead,
The moon-splashed waves exult.

At dawn the ship trembles, turns
In a wide arc to back
Shuddering up the grey lough
Past lightship and buoy,
Slipway and dry dock
Where a naked bulb burns;

And I step ashore in a fine rain
To a city so changed
By five years of war
I scarcely recognize
The places I grew up in,
The faces that try to explain.

But the hills are still the same
Grey-blue above Belfast.
Perhaps if I'd stayed behind
And lived it bomb by bomb
I might have grown up at last
And learnt what is meant by home.

58

Leaves

The prisoners of infinite choice
Have built their house
In a field below the wood
And are at peace.

It is autumn, and dead leaves
On their way to the river
Scratch like birds at the windows
Or tick on the road.

Somewhere there is an afterlife
Of dead leaves,
A stadium filled with an infinite
Rustling and sighing.

Somewhere in the heaven
Of lost futures
The lives we might have led
Have found their own fulfilment.

Father-in-Law

While your widow clatters water into a kettle
You lie at peace in your southern grave—
A sea captain who died at sea, almost.
Lost voyager, what would you think of me,
Husband of your fair daughter but impractical?
You stare from the mantelpiece, a curious ghost
In your peaked cap, as we sit down to tea.
The bungalows still signal to the sea,

59

Rain wanders the golf course as in your day,
The river flows past the distillery
And a watery sun shines on Portballintrae.

I think we would have had a lot in common—
Alcohol and the love of one woman
Certainly; but I failed the eyesight test
When I tried for the Merchant Navy,
And lapsed into this lyric lunacy.
When you lost your balance like Li Po
They found unfinished poems in your sea-chest.

Homage to Malcolm Lowry

For gear your typewriter and an old rugby boot,
The voyage started, clearly, when you were born
That danced those empty bottles. When you set out
On a round-the-cosmos trip with the furious Muse
Or lay sweating on a hotel bed in Vera Cruz,
Did you not think you had left that pool astern
Where a soul might bathe and be clean or slake its
                                                  drought?
In any case, your deportment in those seas
Was faultless. Lightning-blind, you, tempest-torn
At the poles of our condition, did not confuse
The Gates of Ivory with the Gates of Horn.

Going Home
for Douglas Dunn

Why we died
Remains a mystery,
One we shall never solve.

The recipes, nursery rhymes
And archaic ailments
Of a foreclosed species—

Only a misleading fraction
Will survive on file
To show we could crack a smile.

Only an unrepresentative sample
Will persist on tape
To show what we meant by hope.

Extraordinary people
We were in our time,
How we lived in our time

As if blindfold
Or not wholly serious,
Inventing names for things

To propitiate silence.
It is silence we hug now
In the indigestible

Dawn mist which clings
All afternoon
To the south bank of the Humber—

For ours is the afterlife
Of the unjudgeable,
Of the desolate and free

Who come over
Twice daily from Hull
Disguised as shift workers

And vanish for ever
With a whisper of soles
Under a cindery sky,

The sort of sky
That broke the hearts
Of the foundered legionaries.

Like them we are
Spirits here
With our lunch boxes and

Papers of manumission,
Our speechless debarkations
Without zest or issue.

A pale light wanes
At the pierhead
As if to guide us home

To the blank Elysium
Predicated on our
Eschewal of metaphysics,

A sunken barge rots
In the mud beach
As if finally to discredit

A residual poetry of
Leavetaking and homecoming,
Of work and sentiment;

For this is the last
Homecoming, the end
Of the rainbow—

And the pubs are shut.
There are no
Buses till morning.

The Snow Party
for Louis Asekoff

Bashō, coming
To the city of Nagoya,
Is asked to a snow party.

There is a tinkling of china
And tea into china;
There are introductions.

Then everyone
Crowds to the window
To watch the falling snow.

Snow is falling on Nagoya
And farther south
On the tiles of Kyōto.

Eastward, beyond Irago,
It is falling
Like leaves on the cold sea.

Elsewhere they are burning
Witches and heretics
In the boiling squares,

Thousands have died since dawn
In the service
Of barbarous kings;

But there is silence
In the houses of Nagoya
And the hills of Ise.

The Last of the Fire Kings

I want to be
Like the man who descends
At two milk churns

With a bulging
String bag and vanishes
Where the lane turns,

Or the man
Who drops at night
From a moving train

And strikes out over the fields
Where fireflies glow
Not knowing a word of the language.

Either way, I am
Through with history—
Who lives by the sword

Dies by the sword.
Last of the fire kings, I shall
Break with tradition and

Die by my own hand
Rather than perpetuate
The barbarous cycle.

Five years I have reigned
During which time
I have lain awake each night

And prowled by day
In the sacred grove
For fear of the usurper,

Perfecting my cold dream
Of a place out of time,
A palace of porcelain

Where the frugivorous
Inheritors recline
In their rich fabrics
Far from the sea.

But the fire-loving
People, rightly perhaps,
Will not countenance this,

Demanding that I inhabit,
Like them, a world of
Sirens, bin-lids
And bricked-up windows—

Not to release them
From the ancient curse
But to die their creature and be thankful.

The North African Campaign

'I was here before but I lost last time.'
A light wind touches the dust
Of my confidence and dismay
And is almost like voices.
Stout lads, they are at peace now
In the heaven of the Carthaginians
Watching the contemporary
Elephants at work on the holy places.

The Golden Bough

What will be left after
The twilight of cities,
The flowers of fire,
Will be the soft
Vegetables where our
Politics were conceived.

When we give back
The cleared counties
To the first forest,
The hills to the hills,
The reclaimed mudflats
To the vigilant sea,

There will be silence, then
A sigh of waking
As from a long dream.
Once more I shall rise early
And plough my country
By first light,

At noon lie down
In a warm field,
My head in the shade,
And after midnight
Fish for stars
In the dark waters.

Once more I shall worship
The moon, make gods
Of clay, gods of stone,
And celebrate
In a world of waste
Their deaths and their return.

The Antigone Riddle

Elocution, logic, political science,
Antibiotics, do-it-yourself,
And a plover flops in his oil slick.

Shy minerals contract at the sound of his voice,
Cod point in silence when his bombers pass,
And the windfall waits
In silence for his departure
Before it drops in
Silence to the long grass.

The Facts of Life
after Cavafy

I will not be known by what I did or said.
The facts of life conspired
To block action, tie tongue. Nothing
Came out as I intended.

No, look for my secret
In the lost grin,
The poker-faced elision.

Reborn in the ideal society
I shall act and speak
With a freedom denied me
By the life we know.

Nostalgias

The chair squeaks in a high wind,
Rain falls from its branches,
The kettle yearns for the
Mountain, the soap for the sea.
In a tiny stone church
On the desolate headland
A lost tribe is singing 'Abide With Me'.

68

The Mute Phenomena
after Nerval

Your great mistake is to disregard the satire
Bandied among the mute phenomena.
Be strong if you must, your brusque hegemony
Means fuck-all to the somnolent sunflower
Or the extinct volcano. What do you know
Of the revolutionary theories advanced
By turnips, or the sex-life of cutlery?
Everything is susceptible, Pythagoras said so.

An ordinary common-or-garden brick wall, the kind
For talking to or banging your head on,
Resents your politics and bad draughtsmanship.
God is alive and lives under a stone.
Already in a lost hub-cap is conceived
The ideal society which will replace our own.

Matthew V. 29-30

Lord, mine eye offended, so I plucked it out.
   Imagine my chagrin
when the offence continued.
   So I plucked out
the other; but the offence continued.

In the dark now, and working by touch,
   I shaved my head.
(The offence continued.)
   Removed an ear,
another, dispatched the nose.
   The offence continued.
Imagine my chagrin.

Next, in long strips, the skin—
   razored the tongue, the toes,
the personal nitty-gritty.
   The offence continued.

But now, the thing finding its own momentum,
   the more so since
      the offence continued,
I entered upon a prolonged course
   of lobotomy and vivisection,
      reducing the self
to a rubble of organs, a wreckage of bones
   in the midst of which, somewhere,
      the offence continued.

Quicklime, then, for the calcium, paraquat
   for the unregenerate offal;
a spreading of topsoil,
   a ploughing of this
      and a sowing of it with barley.

Paraffin for the records of birth, flu
   and abortive scholarship,
for the whimsical postcards, the cheques
   dancing like hail,
the surviving copies of poems published
   and unpublished; a scalpel
for the casual turns of phrase engraved
   on the minds of others;
an aerosol for the stray thoughts
   hanging in air,
for the people who breathed them in.

Sadly, therefore, deletion of the many people
    from their desks, beds, breakfasts,
        buses and catamarans;
deletion of their machinery and architecture,
    all evidence whatever
    of civility and reflection,
        of laughter and tears.

Destruction of all things on which
    that reflection fed,
        of vegetable and bird;
        erosion of all rocks
    from the holiest mountain
        to the least stone;
        evaporation of all seas,
the extinction of heavenly bodies—
        until, at last, offence
        was not to be found
    in that silence without bound.

Only then was I fit for human society.

The Mayo Tao
for Eugene Lambe

I have abandoned the dream kitchens for a low fire
   and a prescriptive
      literature of the spirit.
A storm snores on the desolate sea.

The nearest shop is four miles away.
   When I walk there
      through the shambles of the morning
for tea and firelighters,
   the mountain paces me
      in a snow-lit silence.

My days are spent in conversation
   with stags and blackbirds;
      at night fox and badger
         gather at my door.

I have stood for hours watching
   a salmon doze
      in the tea-gold dark,
for weeks watching a spider weave
   in a pale light, for months
listening to the sob-story
   of a stone on the road—
      the best, most monotonous
sob-story I have ever heard.

I am an expert on frost crystals
   and the silence of crickets,
a confidant of the stinking shore,
   the stars in the mud.

(There is an immanence in these things
   which drives me, despite
      my scepticism, almost
   to the point of speech—
      like sunlight cleaving
   the lake mist at morning
or when tepid water runs cold at last from the tap.)

I have been working for years
   on a four-line poem
      about the life of a leaf.
I think it may come out right this winter.

The Apotheosis of Tins

Having spent the night in a sewer of precognition,
   consoled by moon-glow, air-chuckle
      and the retarded
         pathos of mackerel,
we wake among shoe-laces and white wood
   to a raw wind and the cries of gulls.

Deprived of use, we are safe now
   from the historical nightmare
      and may give our attention at last
         to things of the spirit,
noticing for example the consanguinity
   of sand and stone,
      how they are thicker than water,
and the pebbles shorter than their shadows.

This is the terminal democracy
    of hatbox and crab,
        of hock and Windowlene.
            It is always rush-hour.
If we have learnt one thing from our desertion
    by the sour smudge on the horizon,
        from the erosion of labels,
            it is the value of self-definition.
No one, not even the poet
    whose shadow halts above us after
        dawn and before dark,
            will have our trust.
We resist your patronage, your reflective leisure.

Promoted artifacts by the dereliction
    of our creator, and greater now
        than the sum of his skills,
we shall be with you while there are beaches.

Imperishable by-products of the perishable will,
    we shall lie like skulls
        in the hands of soliloquists.
The longest queues in the science museum
    will form at our last homes
        saying, 'Think now,

        what an organic relation
        of art to life
    in the dawn; what saintly
devotion to the notion of permanence
    in the flux of sensation
        and crisis, perhaps
            we can learn from them.'

74

A Refusal to Mourn

He lived in a small farmhouse
At the edge of a new estate.
The trim gardens crept
To his door, and car engines
Woke him before dawn
On dark winter mornings.

All day there was silence
In the bright house. The clock
Ticked on the kitchen shelf,
Cinders moved in the grate,
And a warm briar gurgled
When the old man talked to himself;

But the doorbell seldom rang
After the milkman went,
And if a coat-hanger
Knocked in an open wardrobe
That was a strange event
To be pondered on for hours

While the wind thrashed about
In the back garden, raking
The roof of the hen-house,
And swept clouds and gulls
Eastwards over the lough
With its flap of tiny sails.

Once a week he would visit
An old shipyard crony,
Inching down to the road
And the blue country bus
To sit and watch sun-dappled
Branches whacking the windows

While the long evening shed
Weak light in his empty house,
On the photographs of his dead
Wife and their six children
And the Missions to Seamen angel
In flight above the bed.

'I'm not long for this world'
Said he on our last evening,
'I'll not last the winter',
And grinned, straining to hear
Whatever reply I made;
And died the following year.

In time the astringent rain
Of those parts will clean
The words from his gravestone
In the crowded cemetery
That overlooks the sea
And his name be mud once again

And his boilers lie like tombs
In the mud of the sea bed
Till the next ice age comes
And the earth he inherited
Is gone like Neanderthal Man
And no records remain.

But the secret bred in the bone
On the dawn strand survives
In other times and lives,
Persisting for the unborn
Like a claw-print in concrete
After the bird has flown.

Postcards

1 Málaga
Waking alone at dead of night
in a silent house, I lay
listening to a dog bark
in the dark country;
with the star-lit stones,
the reflective spider,
the grapes dreaming
of the wine one day.

2 Patmos
It is long since I was a herdsman
studying the punctual
haemorrhage of sea and sky,
the galaxies of dust;
since I was a bondsman,
patient for nightfall
and the ringing tone
of moonlight on white stone.

The Banished Gods

Near the headwaters of the longest river
   There is a forest clearing,
     A dank, misty place
   Where light stands in columns
And birds sing with a noise like paper tearing.

Far from land, far from the trade routes,
   In an unbroken dream-time
     Of penguin and whale,
   The seas sigh to themselves
Reliving the days before the days of sail.

Where the wires end the moor seethes in silence,
   Scattered with scree, primroses,
     Feathers and faeces.
   It shelters the hawk and hears
In dreams the forlorn cries of lost species.

It is here that the banished gods are in hiding,
   Here they sit out the centuries
     In stone, water
   And the hearts of trees,
Lost in a reverie of their own natures—

Of zero-growth economics and seasonal change
   In a world without cars, computers
     Or chemical skies,
   Where thought is a fondling of stones
And wisdom a five-minute silence at moonrise.

A Disused Shed in Co. Wexford

Let them not forget us, the weak souls among the asphodels.—Seferis, *Mythistorema*

for J. G. Farrell

Even now there are places where a thought might grow—
Peruvian mines, worked out and abandoned
To a slow clock of condensation,
An echo trapped for ever, and a flutter
Of wildflowers in the lift-shaft,
Indian compounds where the wind dances
And a door bangs with diminished confidence,
Lime crevices behind rippling rainbarrels,
Dog corners for bone burials;
And in a disused shed in Co. Wexford,

Deep in the grounds of a burnt-out hotel,
Among the bathtubs and the washbasins
A thousand mushrooms crowd to a keyhole.
This is the one star in their firmament
Or frames a star within a star.
What should they do there but desire?
So many days beyond the rhododendrons
With the world waltzing in its bowl of cloud,
They have learnt patience and silence
Listening to the rooks querulous in the high wood.

They have been waiting for us in a foetor
Of vegetable sweat since civil war days,
Since the gravel-crunching, interminable departure
Of the expropriated mycologist.
He never came back, and light since then
Is a keyhole rusting gently after rain.

Spiders have spun, flies dusted to mildew
And once a day, perhaps, they have heard something—
A trickle of masonry, a shout from the blue
Or a lorry changing gear at the end of the lane.

There have been deaths, the pale flesh flaking
Into the earth that nourished it;
And nightmares, born of these and the grim
Dominion of stale air and rank moisture.
Those nearest the door grow strong—
'Elbow room! Elbow room!'
The rest, dim in a twilight of crumbling
Utensils and broken flower-pots, groaning
For their deliverance, have been so long
Expectant that there is left only the posture.

A half century, without visitors, in the dark—
Poor preparation for the cracking lock
And creak of hinges. Magi, moonmen,
Powdery prisoners of the old regime,
Web-throated, stalked like triffids, racked by drought
And insomnia, only the ghost of a scream
At the flash-bulb firing squad we wake them with
Shows there is life yet in their feverish forms.
Grown beyond nature now, soft food for worms,
They lift frail heads in gravity and good faith.

They are begging us, you see, in their wordless way,
To do something, to speak on their behalf
Or at least not to close the door again.
Lost people of Treblinka and Pompeii!
'Save us, save us,' they seem to say,
'Let the god not abandon us
Who have come so far in darkness and in pain.
We too had our lives to live.
You with your light meter and relaxed itinerary,
Let not our naive labours have been in vain!'

Ford Manor
Non sapei tu che qui è l'uom felice?

Even on the quietest days the distant
Growl of cars remains persistent,
Reaching us in this airy box
We share with the field-mouse and the fox;
But she drifts in maternity blouses
Among crack-paned greenhouses—
A smiling Muse come back to life,
Part child, part mother, and part wife.

Even on the calmest nights the fitful
Prowl of planes is seldom still
Where Gatwick tilts to guide them home
From Tokyo, New York or Rome;
Yet even today the earth disposes
Bluebells, roses and primroses,
The dawn throat-whistle of a thrush
Deep in the dripping lilac bush.

Penshurst Place
And if these pleasures may thee move . . .

The bright drop quivering on a thorn
In the rich silence after rain,
Lute music from the orchard aisles,
The paths ablaze with daffodils,
Intrigue and venery in the air
A l'ombre des jeunes filles en fleurs,
The iron hand and the velvet glove—
Come live with me and be my love.

A pearl face, numinously bright,
Shining in silence of the night,
A muffled crash of smouldering logs,
Bad dreams of courtiers and of dogs,
The Spanish ships around Kinsale,
The screech owl and the nightingale,
The falcon and the turtle dove—
Come live with me and be my love.

Three Poems after Jaccottet

1 The Voice

What is it that sings when the other voices are silent?
Whose is that pure, deaf voice, that sibilant song?
Is it down the road on a snow-covered lawn
or close at hand, aware of an audience?
This is the mysterious first bird of dawn.
Do you hear the voice increase in volume
and, as a March wind quickens the creaking trees,
sing mildly to us without fear,
content in the fact of death? Do you hear?
What does it sing in the grey dawn? Nobody knows;
but the voice is audible only to those
whose hearts are emptied of property and desire.

2 Ignorance

The older I get the more ignorant I become;
the longer I live the less I possess or control.
All I have is a little space, snow-dark
or glittering—never inhabited.
Where is the giver, the guide, the guardian?
I sit in my room and am silent. Silence
comes in like a servant to tidy things up
while I wait for the lies to disperse.
And what remains to this dying man
that so well prevents him from dying?
What does he find to say to the four walls?
I hear him talking still, and his words
come in with the dawn, imperfectly formed:
'Love, like fire, can only reveal its clarity
on the failure and the beauty of ashen forests.'

3 *The Gipsies*

There are fires under the trees.
Low voices speak to the sleeping nations
from the fringes of cities.

If, short-lived souls that we are,
we pass silently
on the dark road tonight,
it is for fear you should die,
perpetual murmur
around the hidden light.

Surrey Poems

1 *Midsummer*

Today the longest day and the people have gone.
The sun concentrates on the kitchen garden
with the bright intensity of June.
The birds we heard singing at dawn
are dozing among the leaves
while a faint soap waits its turn
in a blue sky, strange to the afternoon—
one eye on the pasture where cows roam
and one on the thin line between land
and sea, where the quietest waves
will break there when the people have gone home.

2 *Field Bath*
Ancient bathtub in the fallow field—
midges, brown depths where once
a drift of rainbow suds,
rosewater and lavender.
Now cow faces, clouds,
starlight, nobody there.

Nobody there for days and nights
but my own curious thoughts
out there on their own
in a rainstorm or before dawn
peering over the rim
and sending nothing back to my warm room.

3 *The Wood*
A frightened shriek in the wood,
the whining saw spins free,
and the puff of dust
lost in the mist
is the hurt spirit escaping
from the throat of the stricken tree.

4 *Dry Hill*
The grass falls silent and the trees cease
when my shoes go swishing there.
Vetch, thyme, cowslip,
whatever your names are,
there is no need for fear—
I am only looking. Perhaps
that is what you are afraid of?

Did I tell you about my grandparents,
how they slaved all their lives
and for what? Did I tell you
about the lot of women,
the eyes of children?
Did I tell you the one about?

Please yourselves, at least I tried;
I have a right to be here too.
Maybe not like you—
like the birds,
say, or the wind blowing through.

Soles

'I caught four soles this morning'
said the man with the beard;
cloud shifted and a sun-
shaft pierced the sea.
Fisher of soles, did you reflect
the water you walked on
contains so very many souls,
the living and the dead,
you could never begin to count them?

Somewhere a god waits,
rod in hand,
to add you to their number.

Jet Trail

Jet trail and early moon—
  A golden star pierces
The pale empyrean;
  The white flock disperses.

The white flock disperses
  Watched by an early moon.
The star diminishes;
  It will be dark soon.

It will be dark soon
  On holly and oak tree.
Seat belts are undone
  Above a glittering sea.

Above a glittering sea
  The pale empyrean,
A golden star silently
  Watched by an early moon.

Autobiographies
for Maurice Leitch

1 The Home Front
While the frozen armies trembled
At the gates of Stalingrad
They took me home in a taxi
And laid me in my cot,
And there I slept again
With siren and black-out;

And slept under the stairs
Beside the light meter
When bombs fell on the city;
So I never saw the sky
Filled with a fiery glow,
Searchlights roaming the stars.

But I do remember one time
(I must have been four then)
Being held up to the window
For a victory parade—
Soldiers, sailors and airmen
Lining the Antrim Road;

And, later, hide-and-seek
Among the air-raid shelters,
The last ration coupons,
Oranges and bananas,
Forage caps and badges
And packets of Lucky Strike.

Gracie Fields on the radio!
Americans in the art-deco
Milk bars! The released Jews
Blinking in shocked sunlight . . .
A male child in a garden
Clutching *The Empire News*.

2 *The Lost Girls*
'In ancient shadows and twilights
Where childhood had strayed'
I ran round in the playground
Of Skegoneill Primary School
During the lunch hour,
Pretending to be a plane.

For months I would dawdle home
At a respectful distance
Behind the teacher's daughter,
Eileen Boyd, who lived
In a house whose back garden
Was visible from my window.

I watched her on summer evenings,
A white dress picking flowers,
Her light, graceful figure
Luminous and remote.
We never exchanged greetings:
Her house was bigger than ours.

She married an older man
And went to live in Kenya.
Perhaps she is there still
Complaining about 'the natives'.
It would be nice to know;
But who can re-live their lives?

Eileen Boyd, Hazel and Heather
Thompson, Patricia King—
The lost girls in a ring
On a shadowy school playground
Like the nymphs dancing together
In the 'Allegory of Spring'.

3 The Last Resort
Salad-and-sand sandwiches
And dead gulls on the beach;
Ice-cream in the Arcadia,
Rain lashing the windows;
Dull days in the harbour,
Sunday mornings in church.

One lost July fortnight
In the Strandmore Hotel
I watched the maid climb
The stairs, and went to my room
Quivering with excitement,
Randy for the first time.

Years later, the same dim
Resort has grown dimmer
As if some centrifugal
Force, summer by summer,
Has moved it ever further
From an imagined centre.

The small hotels are randy
For custom; but the risen
People are playing football
On the sands of Tenerife,
Far from the unrelaxing
Scenes of sectarian strife.

Yet the place really existed
And still can crack a smile
Should a sunbeam pick out
Your grimy plastic cup
And consecrate your vile
Bun with its parting light.

4 The Bicycle
There was a bicycle, a fine
Raleigh with five gears
And racing handlebars.
It stood at the front door
Begging to be mounted;
The frame shone in the sun.

I became like a character
In *The Third Policeman*, half
Human, half bike, my life
A series of dips and ridges,
Happiness a free-wheeling
Past fragrant hawthorn hedges.

Cape and sou'wester streamed
With rain when I rode to school
Side-tracking the bus routes.
Night after night I dreamed
Of valves, pumps, sprockets,
Reflectors and repair kits.

Soon there were long rides
In the country, wet week-ends
Playing snap in the kitchens
Of mountain youth hostels,
Day-runs to Monaghan,
Rough and exotic roads.

It went with me to Dublin
Where I sold it the same winter;
But its wheels still sing
In the memory, stars that turn
About an eternal centre,
The bright spokes glittering.

Light Music

The glow-worm shows the matin
  to be near . . .

1 Architecture
Twinkletoes in the ballroom,
light music in space.

2 History
The blinking puddles
reflected daylong
twilights of misery.

Smoke rose in silence
to the low sky.

3 Negatives
Gulls in a rain-dark cornfield,
crows on a sunlit sea.

4 North Sea
The terminal light of beaches,
pebbles speckled with oil;
old tins at the tide-line
where a gull blinks on a pole.

5 Aesthetics
Neither the tearful taper
nor the withered wick,
that sickly crowd;
but the single bright
landing light
ghosting an iodine cloud.

6 *Please*
I built my house
in a forest far
from the venal roar.

Somebody please
beat a path
to my door.

7 *Rory*
He leads me into
a grainy twilight
of old photographs.

The sun is behind us,
his shadow in mine.

8 *Spring*
Dawnlight pearling the branches,
petals freckling the mould,
and the stereo birds.

It is time for the nymphs,
a glimpse of skin in the woods.

9 *Twilight*
A stone at the roadside
watches snow fall
on the silent gate-lodge.

Later the gate shuts
with a clanging of bars;
the stone is one with the stars.

10 Midnight
Torchlight swept
the firmament,
chords softly crashed.

But the hedgerows
quiver aghast
when our headlights pass.

11 Astronaut
Give me some information
on China and Greece;
the only place
I ever went was the moon.

12 Byzantium
Moth thought of masonry,
daylight mured
from the wine bins.

Silent in one corner
the gleam of a dead star.

13 Joyce in Paris
This town a lantern
hung for lovers
in a dark wood
says the blind man.

14 Mozart
The Clarinet Concerto
in A, K.622;
the second movement.

Turn it up
so they can hear
on the other planets.

15 Rembrandt
The sun went searching
on various surfaces,
alighting finally
on a human face—
my own, flinching
visibly from its gaze.

16 Morphology
Beans and foetuses,
brains and cauliflowers;
in a shaft of sunlight
a dust of stars.

17 Come In
The steel regrets the lock,
a word will open the rock,
the wood awaits your knock.

18 Magritte

The thing deserts the word,
weary of categories;
in search of other seas
the bird forsakes the bird.

Now what pale thighs
open the door in the cloud?

19 Elpenor

Edacity in the palace
and in the sandy timber
of my crumbling monument,
its lengthening shadow
pointing towards home.

20 October

The fields dark under
a gunmetal sky, and one
tiny farm shining
in a patch of sunlight
as if singled out
for benediction.

21 East Strand

Tedium of sand and sea
then at the white rocks
a little girl fleetingly,
blazer and ankle socks.

Sand drifts from the dunes
like driven smoke, and one
gull attentive to my walk
occludes the winter sun.

22 *Donegal*
The vast clouds migrate
above turf-stacks
and a dangling gate.

A tiny bike squeaks
into the wind.

23 *Rogue Leaf*
Believe it or not
I hung on all winter
outfacing wind and snow.

Now that spring
comes and the birds sing
I am letting go.

24 *Revelation*
A colour the fish know
we do not know, so
long have we been ashore.

When that colour
shines in the rainbow
there will be no more sea.

25 *Flying*
A wand of sunlight
touches the rush-hour
like the finger of heaven.

A land of cumulus
seen from above
is the life to come.

The Return
for John Hewitt

I am saying goodbye to the trees,
The beech, the cedar, the elm,
The mild woods of these parts
Misted with car exhaust,
And sawdust, and the last
Gasps of the poisoned nymphs.

I have watched girls walking
And children playing under
Lilac and rhododendron,
And me flicking my ash
Into the rose bushes
As if I owned the place;

As if the trees responded
To my ignorant admiration
Before dawn when the branches
Glitter at first light,
Or later on when the finches
Disappear for the night;

And often thought if I lived
Long enough in this house
I would turn into a tree
Like somebody in Ovid
—A small tree certainly
But a tree nonetheless—

Perhaps befriend the oak,
The chestnut and the yew,
Become a home for birds,
A shelter for the nymphs,
And gaze out over the downs
As if I belonged here too.

But where I am going the trees
Are few and far between.
No richly forested slopes,
Not for a long time,
And few winking woodlands;
There are no nymphs to be seen.

Out there you would look in vain
For a rose bush; but find,
Rooted in stony ground,
A last stubborn growth
Battered by constant rain
And twisted by the sea-wind

With nothing to recommend it
But its harsh tenacity
Between the blinding windows
And the forests of the sea,
As if its very existence
Were a reason to continue.

Crone, crow, scarecrow,
Its worn fingers scrabbling
At a torn sky, it stands
On the edge of everything
Like a burnt-out angel
Raising petitionary hands.

Grotesque by day, at twilight
An almost tragic figure
Of anguish and despair,
It merges into the funeral
Cloud-continent of night
As if it belongs there.

Lingfield-Coleraine, 1977

The Chinese Restaurant in Portrush

Before the holidaymakers comes the spring
Softening the sharp air of the coast
In time for the first 'invasion'.
Today the place is as it might have been,
Gentle and almost hospitable. A girl
Strides past the Northern Counties Hotel,
Light-footed, swinging a book-bag,
And the doors that were shut all winter
Against the north wind and the sea-mist
Lie open to the street, where one
By one the gulls go window-shopping
And an old wolfhound dozes in the sun.

While I sit with my paper and prawn chow-mein
Under a framed photograph of Hong Kong
The proprietor of the Chinese restaurant
Stands at the door as if the world were young
Watching the first yacht hoist a sail—
An ideogram on sea-cloud—and the light
Of heaven upon the mountains of Donegal;
And whistles a little tune, dreaming of home.

The Blackbird

One morning in the month of June
I was coming out of this door
And found myself in a garden,
A sanctuary of light and air
Transplanted from the Hesperides,
No sound of machinery anywhere,
When from a bramble bush a hidden
Blackbird suddenly gave tongue,
Its diffident, resilient song
Breaking the silence of the seas.

The Old Snaps

I keep your old snaps in my bottom drawer—
The icons of a more than personal love.
Look, three sisters out of Chekhov
('When will we ever go to Moscow?')
Ranged on the steps of the school-house
Where their mother is head teacher,
Out on the rocks, or holding down their hair
In a high wind on a North Antrim shore.

Later, yourself alone among sand-hills
Striking a slightly fictional pose,
Life-ready and impervious to harm
In your wind-blown school uniform
While the salt sea air fills
Your young body with ozone
And fine sand trickles into your shoes.
I think I must have known you even then.

We went to Moscow, and we will again.
Meanwhile we walk on the strand
And smile as if for the first time
While the children play in the sand.
We have never known a worse winter
But the old snaps are always there,
Framed for ever in your heart and mine
Where no hands can twist or tear.

The Attic
for John and Evelyn Montague

Under the night window
   A dockyard fluorescence,
Muse-light on the city—
   A world of heightened sense.

At work in your attic
   Up here under the roof—
Listen, can you hear me
   Turning over a new leaf?

Silent by ticking lamplight
   I stare at the blank spaces,
Reflecting the composure
   Of patient surfaces—

I who know nothing
   Scribbling on the off-chance,
Darkening the white page,
   Cultivating my ignorance.

The Poet in Residence
after Corbière

A ruined convent on the Breton coast—
Gathering-place for wind and mist,
Where the donkeys of Finistère
Sheltered against the ivied walls,
Masonry pitted with such gaping holes
There was no knowing which one was the door.

Lonely but upright, in undiminished pride,
The old hag of the countryside,
Roof like a hat askew, it stood
Remembering its past—a den
For smugglers and night-wanderers now,
For stray dogs, rats, lovers and excisemen.

A feral poet lived in the one-eyed tower,
His wings clipped, having settled there
Among watchful and lugubrious owls.
He respected their rights however,
He, the only owl who paid—
A thousand francs a year 'and a new door'.

The locals he ignored, though not they him.
Sharp eyes saw from the road below
Where he dithered at a window.
The priest was sure he was a leper
But the mayor said, 'What can I do?
He's probably a foreigner of some kind.'

The women, though, were not slow to discover
That this barely visible recluse
Shared the place with a lover
Whom he referred to as his 'Muse'—
Parisians, no doubt, the pair of them!
But she lay low, and the storm blew over.

He was, in fact, one of life's fugitives,
An amateur hermit blown in with the leaves
Who had lived too long by a southern sea.
Pursued by doctors and taxmen
He had come here in search of peace,
To die alone or live in contumacy—

An artist or philosopher, after a fashion,
Who chose to live beyond the pale.
He had his hammock, his barrel-organ,
His little dog Fidèle
And, no less faithful, gentle and grave as he,
A lifelong intimate he called Ennui.

He dreamed his life, his dream the tide that flows
Rattling among the stones, the tide that ebbs.
Sometimes he stood there as if listening—
For what? For the wind to rise,
For the sea to sing?
Or for some half-forgotten voice? Who knows?

Does he know himself? Up there on the exposed
Roof of himself, does he forget how soon
And how completely death unmakes
The dead? He, restless ghost,
Is it perhaps his own lost
Contumacious spirit that he seeks?

Not far, not far, she after whom you bell,
Stag of St Hubert! All may yet be well!
. . . A door banged in his head
And he heard the slow tread of hexameters . . .

Not knowing how to live, he learned how to survive
And, not knowing how to die, he wrote:

'My love,
I write, therefore I am. When I said goodbye
To life, it was you I was saying goodbye to—
You who wept for me so that I wanted
To stay and weep beside you. However
It's too late now, the die is cast.
Oh yes, I'm still here, but as if erased.
I am dying slowly into legend;
Spiders spin in the brain where a star burned.

'Come and help me die; from your room
You'll be able to see my harvest fields
(A few firs shivering in the wind)
And the wild heather in full bloom
(Well, bundled around the fireplace).
You can gulp your fill of the sea air
(It's nearly taking the roof off)
And climb to sleep by a golden stair
(Lit by a single candle)
While the sea murmurs of shipwrecks—
Tenebrae for the wild ducks.

'Like *Paul et Virginie*, if that's your choice,
We'll lose ourselves in a lost paradise.
Or like Robinson Crusoe, no problem—
The rain has made an island of my kingdom.
Moreover, you need not fear solitude
What with the poacher and the exciseman.

And the nights! Nights for orgies in the tower!
Romeo nights that no sun rises on!
Nights of the nightingale in the gale!
Can you hear my Aeolian door squeal
And the rats whirl in the attic?

'You inhabit my dreams and my day-dreams; over
Everything, like a spirit, you hover.
You are my solitude, my owls
And my weathercock; the wind howls
Your name when my shutter
Shakes; and the shadow thrown
For an instant on the bare wall is yours;
Yet when I turn my head it disappears.
A knock at the door! Is that
Your knock there, calling me? No, only a rat.

'I've taken my lyre and my barrel-organ
To serenade you—ridiculous!
Come and cry if I've made you laugh,
Come and laugh if I've made you cry.
Come and play at misery
Taken from life: "Love in a Cottage"!
It rains in my hearth, it rains fire in my heart;
And now my fire is dead, and I have no more light . . .'

His lamp went out; he opened the shutter.
The sun rose; he gazed at his letter,
Laughed and then tore it up . . .

    The little bits of white
Looked, in the mist, like gulls in flight.

Everything Is Going To Be All Right

How should I not be glad to contemplate
the clouds clearing beyond the dormer window
and a high tide reflected on the ceiling?
There will be dying, there will be dying,
but there is no need to go into that.
The poems flow from the hand unbidden
and the hidden source is the watchful heart.
The sun rises in spite of everything
and the far cities are beautiful and bright.
I lie here in a riot of sunlight
watching the day break and the clouds flying.
Everything is going to be all right.

Heraclitus on Rivers

Nobody steps into the same river twice.
The same river is never the same
Because that is the nature of water.
Similarly your changing metabolism
Means that you are no longer you.
The cells die; and the precise
Configuration of the heavenly bodies
When she told you she loved you
Will not come again in this lifetime.

You will tell me that you have executed
A monument more lasting than bronze;
But even bronze is perishable.
Your best poem, you know the one I mean,
The very language in which the poem
Was written, and the idea of language,
All these things will pass away in time.

The Window

```
woodwoodwoodwoodwoodwoodwoodwood
io                                        oo
n o                                      o w
d    d                                   w    i
o    w                                   o    n
w    o                                   o    d
i    o                                   d    o
n    d                                   w    w
d    w                                   o    i
o    o                                   o    n
w    o                                   d    d
i    d                                   w    o
n    w                  wind             o    w
d    o                                   o    i
o    o                                   d    n
w    d                                   w    d
i    w                                   o    o
n    d                                   w    w
d o                                      o    i
oo                                           on
woodwoodwoodwoodwoodwoodwoodwood
dwoodwoodwoodwoodwoodwoodwoodwoodw
odwoodwoodwoodwoodwoodwoodwoodwoodwo
```

The Sea in Winter

Nous ne sommes pas au monde;
la vraie vie est absente.—
　　　　　Rimbaud, *Une Saison en Enfer*

for Desmond O'Grady

Desmond, what of the blue nights,
The ultramarines and violets
Of your white island in the south,
'Far-shining star of dark-blue earth',
And the boat-lights in the tiny port
Where we drank so much retsina?
Up here where the air is thinner,
In a draughty bungalow in Portstewart

Beside my 'distant northern sea',
I imagine a moon of Asia Minor
Bright on your nightly industry.
Sometimes, rounding the cliff top
At dusk, under the convent wall,
And finding the little town lit up
As if for some island festival,
I pretend not to be here at all;

That the shop fronts along the prom,
Whose fluorescence blinds the foam
And shingle, are the dancing lights
Of Paros—those calescent nights!—
That these frosty pavements are
The stones of that far-shining star;
That the cold, glistening sea-mist
Eclipses Naxos to the east.

But morning scatters down the strand
Relics of last night's gale-force wind.
Far out, the Atlantic faintly breaks,
Seaweed exhales among the rocks,
And fretfully the spent winds fan
The cenotaph and the lifeboat mine.
From door to door the Ormo van
Delivers, while the stars decline.

This is where Jimmy Kennedy wrote
'Red Sails in the Sunset'. Blue
And intimate, Elysian
And neighbourly, the Inishowen
Of Joyce Cary and Red Hugh
Gleams in the distance. On a clear day
You can see Jura and Islay
Severe against the northern sky.

Portstewart, Portrush, Portballintrae—
Un beau pays mal habité,
Policed by rednecks in dark cloth
And roving gangs of tartan youth.
No place for a gentleman like you.
The good, the beautiful and the true
Have a tough time of it; and yet
There *is* that rather obvious sunset,

And a strange poetry of decay
Charms the senile hotels by day,
While in the small hours the rattle
Of a cat knocking over a milk bottle
On a distant doorstep by moonlight
Can set you thinking half the night.
The stars that shone on Nineveh
Shine still on the Harbour Bar.

You too have known the curious sense
Of working on the circumference—
The midnight oil, familiar sea,
Elusive dawn epiphany,
Faith that the trivia doodled here
Will bear their fruit sometime, somewhere;
That the long winter months may bring
Gifts for Diana in the spring.

The sea in winter, where she walks,
Vents its displeasure on the rocks.
The something rotten in the state
Infects the innocent. The spite
Mankind has brought to this infernal
Backwater destroys the soul;
It creeps into the daily life,
Sunders the husband from the wife.

When I returned one year ago
I felt like Tonio Kröger—slow
To come to terms with my own past
Yet knowing I could never cast
Aside the things that made me what,
For better or worse, I am. The upshot?
Chaos and instability,
The cool gaze of the RUC.

Also the prodigal son in *Ghosts*,
Back on the grim, arthritic coasts
Of the cold north, where I found myself
Unnerved, my talents on the shelf,
Slumped in a deckchair, full of pills,
While light died in the choral hills—
On antabuse and mogadon
Recovering, crying out for the sun.

121

Why am I always staring out
Of windows, preferably from a height?
I think the redemptive enterprise
Of water—hold it to the light!—
Yet distance is the vital bond
Between the window and the wind,
While equilibrium demands
A cold eye and deliberate hands.

Sometimes—a deliberate exercise—
I study the tide-warp in the glass,
The wandering raindrops, casual flies;
But still, beyond the shivering grass,
The creamy seas and turbulent skies
Race in the bloodstream where they pass
Like metaphors for human life—
Sex, death, and purgatorial strife.

A fine view may console the heart
With analogues for one kind of art—
Chaste winter-gardens of the sea
Glimmering to infinity;
Yet in those greasy depths will stir
No tengo mas que dar te where
Jehovah blew, and ship by ship
Consigned its ordnance to the deep.

And all the time I have my doubts
About this verse-making. The shouts
Of souls in torment round the town
At closing time make as much sense
And carry as much significance
As these lines carefully set down.
All farts in a biscuit tin, in truth—
Faint cries, sententious or uncouth.

Yet they are most of life, and not
The laid-back metropolitan lot,
The 'great' photographer and the hearty
Critic at the cocktail party.
Most live like these with wire and dust
And dream machinery. My disgust
At their pathetic animation
Merely reflects my own condition;

For I am trapped as much as they
In my own idiom. One day,
Perhaps, the words will find their mark
And leave a brief glow on the dark,
Effect mutations of dead things
Into a form that nearly sings,
Or a quiescent desuetude—
Indolence more than attitude.

And will the year two thousand find
Me still at a window, pen in hand,
Watching long breakers curl on sand
Erosion makes for ever finer?
I hope so, for the sake of these
Subsidized serendipities.
'Ghostlier demarcations, keener
Sounds' are needed more than ever.

To start from scratch, to make it new,
'Forsake the grey skies for the blue',
To find the narrow road to the deep
North the road to Damascus, leap
Before we look! The ideal future
Shines out of our better nature,
Dimly visible from afar:
'The sun is but a morning star'.

In Botticelli's strangely neglected
Drawings for *The Divine Comedy*
Beatrice and the rest proceed
Through a luminous geometry—
Diagrams of that paradise
Each has his vision of. I trace
The future in a colour-scheme,
Colours we scarcely dare to dream.

One day, the day each one conceives—
The day the Dying Gaul revives,
The day the girl among the trees
Strides through our wrecked technologies,
The stones speak out, the rainbow ends,
The wine goes round among the friends,
The lost are found, the parted lovers
Lie at peace beneath the covers.

Meanwhile the given life goes on;
There is nothing new under the sun.
The dogs bark and the caravan
Glides mildly by; and if the dawn
That wakes us now should also find us
Cured of our ancient colour-blindness . . .
I who know nothing go to teach
While a new day crawls up the beach.

Portstewart–Portrush; Oct., 1977–Sept., 1978

Index of First Lines

116